W9-AQZ-506

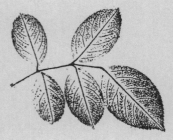

A BOOK OF HOURS

Elizabeth Yates

ART BY CAROL AYMAR ARMSTRONG

UPPER ROOM BOOKS

NASHVILLE

A Book of Hours

© 1976 by Elizabeth Yates
All rights reserved.

Upper Room edition published in 1989. Originally published by Seabury Press.

All scripture quotations are from the King James version of the Bible.

Excerpt from *Jesus Rediscovered* by Malcolm Muggeridge. Copyright © 1969 by Malcolm Muggeridge. Reprinted by permission of Doubleday, a division of Bantam, Doubleday, Dell Publishing Group, Inc. and David Higham Associates, Ltd.

Excerpt from *Reflections on Growing Old* by John LaFarge. Reprinted by permission of Doubleday, a division of Bantam, Doubleday, Dell Publishing Group, Inc. Copyright © 1963 by The America Press.

Excerpt from *Diary of Private Prayer* by John Baillie reproduced by permission of Charles Scribner's Sons, an imprint of Macmillan Publishing Co., and Oxford University Press. Copyright © 1949 Charles Scribner's Sons. Copyright renewed 1977 by Ian Fowler Baillie.

Excerpt from *Meditations of the Heart* by Howard Thurman, originally published by Harper & Row, New York, 1953. Reprinted by Friends United Press, Richmond, Indiana, 1976. Used by permission of the Howard Thurman Estate.

Excerpt from *Tales from the Hasidim: The Early Masters* by Martin Buber. Copyright © 1947 by Schocken Books, New York. Published by Pantheon Books, a division of Random House, Inc. Reprinted by permission of Schocken Books, Inc.

First Upper Room Printing: March, 1989 (5)
ISBN 0-8358-0594-8
Printed in the United States of America

Note

Books of Hours became popular during the late Middle Ages. They were written and designed for the private devotions of the laity and illustrated by exquisitely detailed drawings. Highly individual in character, no two books were exactly alike.

This contemporary Book of Hours is patterned after none of its forebears although inspired by all of them. It is a book designed in and for our own time.

Foreword

One of the monastic disciplines of the Middle Ages was to take the striking of the clock as a reminder to turn thought to God. Perhaps it was easy to respond to that recurrent reminder in a way of life that was God-centered; perhaps it is more difficult now. However, it was a discipline that proved itself; it is one that can still prove itself.

Jeremy Taylor, writing in the 17th century, had this to say—

When the clock strikes, or however else you shall measure the day, it is good to say a short ejaculation every hour, that the parts and returns of devotion may be the measure of your time; and so do also in all the branches of thy sleep, that those spaces which have in them no direct business of the world may be filled with religion.

- 5 -

But why fill these spaces with religion, a word of wide and varied interpretation? Toward what would such a discipline lead?

Howard Thurman, writing in the 20th century, says—

The discipline of prayer is to keep oneself open to God and be ready to respond. The answer comes when there is an inner quickening: a quickening.

Prayer is the means by which we keep ourselves aware of God and open to God's leading. It is a holding, not only when the clock strikes but in all the moments between, as one can still think of a friend while engaged in some activity; as a writer or artist will continue inwardly to develop an idea while outwardly carrying on a routine task.

Brother Lawrence, in his *Practice of the Presence of God*, made his secret plain—

The time of busyness does not with me differ from the time of prayer, and in the noise and clatter of my kitchen, while several persons are at the same time calling for different things, I possess God in as great tranquillity as if I were upon my knees·at the Blessed Sacrament.

In the present pace of life we often feel enslaved by the sweep and rush of time. Seconds move into minutes, minutes pass into hours, hours become days, and where has the time gone? But time is ours to use, to grow with, and when the hours are thought of separately there often seems to be more time in them.

We all have our patterns of living. Some of us work during the day, others during the night; some of us have periods of sleeplessness, others of sudden waking. So in this book there are prayers and meditations for each hour of the twenty-four.

We tend to turn to prayer in extreme moments: great joy, "O, how good God is!" When all human sources have failed, "O, God help me." Anguish, guilt, fear send us to God when no aid is near or, if near, would not understand. But prayer may be so much more: a way of life, a resource, a comfort, a continuing communion.

This continuing communion does not come about without effort. It is an exercise of the spirit that has a discipline of its own. I like to send myself to a dictionary for the actual definition of a word which I have been using rather freely. Webster enlarges my concept of the word discipline: "training which corrects, molds, strengthens, or perfects." There is nothing harsh about that, rather something encouraging. Through training a desired end can be achieved.

I ask myself where would the musician be without the long hours, the constancy of practice? or the writer, working alone, holding to a vision and learning from rejection and disappointment how to perfect that vision? or the ballet dancer? or the doctor? The list lengthens of those who accept a particular discipline because it is training for the work they have chosen to do.

The aim of any discipline of prayer is to become quietly but constantly aware of our relationship to God, not in panic or praise or sudden trial but at all times. The hours come along as reminders, and they may be aided by the striking of a clock, the sound of a bell, or some other hourly recurrence.

Besides employing the time of day to remind us of God we may use those common tasks that arise in the daily round. Some are pleasant and antici-pated, some routine—waking, dressing, prepar-ing meals, going to work, returning. They do not necessarily come on the hour, but as a pause for prayer is made within the hour the assurance of God's nearness is kept alive. Sometimes, too, we can train ourselves to use another kind of reminder—a sudden thrust of loneliness in the empty quiet of a sleepless night, a pang of anger against evil apparently rife, or a twinge of pain. This may be no more than a nuisance, nothing to worry about or worry anyone else about, but thought can be lifted out of the body. "Make sickness itself a prayer," are words from the Mid-dle Ages. There are others whose woes are far greater, whose suffering is more prolonged. This is an occasion to wrap them close in the circle of prayer.

I remember one time in my life when prayer for someone else and the hours of the day became closely interrelated. The son of a friend of mine became desperately ill. She telephoned me early one morning to say that Andrew was not expected to live out the day. He had been in a coma since the long operation. Would I pray for him? To her I said, Yes. To myself I said, Every hour.

I have a small pocket timer that can be set to sound every hour. It makes only a faint hum, but it can be heard and I promised myself to stop whatever I was doing when the hum came and lift my thought to God, holding Andrew in the light and seeing him as ever at one with his Source. After the first reminder, I set the timer for another hour and continued to do so throughout the day, stopping whatever I was doing, wherever I was, when the hum came. Once, in the car, it meant pulling over to the curb and parking; once in a supermarket it meant standing by a shelf as if surveying the products but with eyes closed; several times it was in the quiet of my home. Without anxiety, but with thankfulness, I obeyed the behest.

Late that day I was told that Andrew had died; but I felt sure that his mother would be in touch with me, and the report proved to be a rumor. Every hour, as the hum reminded, I lifted him with invisible hands into the Presence that was his true abiding. Every hour it became easier, more effortless, and the light in which I saw him seemed to become a part of me. At midnight, his mother phoned to say that the crisis had been passed and that Andrew was on the way to recovery.

I asked myself then, as I have many times since: if we did this more often with the issues that imperil our world, what might not happen? This was urgent, of course. But is not anything that is amiss urgent?

Awareness of the hour, with its reminder to be still, gives time for listening. Once I asked a friend of mine who she would be if, for a space of time, she could be someone else. Her reply was immediate: "I would be Mary who sat at the feet of Jesus and listened." Listening is an act of love, an attitude that often must be learned. It is so much easier to talk, to be busy about many things; it is hard to be still and choose the better part. The merest whisper caught inwardly can bring a measure of confidence. In the rush of life it might have gone unheeded; in the quiet it has been heard. I like to recall the words of St. Francis de Sales, "The chief exercise of prayer is to speak to God and to hear God speak in the bottom of our heart."

Prayer, the one language we all can use, is at its deepest a silent language, like that of leaves on a tree, to each other, to the air around them. Tagore said, "Be still, my soul, these great trees are prayers." Whether it be the redwoods in California, a maple stand in New England or a single towering tree, the Gothic principle is there. And, with its upward thrust, a like lifting of the spirit.

One with the trees are their leaves: buds tightly folded during the winter respond to sunshine and rain as the year turns to spring; the surge of new life causes them to open like tiny hands to receive the benison of the elements; opening more to their full size and distinct patterns they perform their function, storing nutrients, purifying the air, providing shade.

Silent the leaves often are and secretive, but just as often they converse as if the secret were too good to be kept to themselves. Whispering in a breeze, rustling, even singing and always in harmony with the wind that plays to them, they give their message. When autumn comes, they have their golden time, then drying and falling they have another function. Swept up or wind driven, their place is close to the soil and their work that of enriching the earth, a far longer process than that which the buds already forming on bare branches have before them.

Keats, in a letter to a friend, said that "if poetry come not as naturally as leaves to a tree it had better not come at all." I paraphrase those words to say that prayer should come to us as naturally as leaves to a tree.

THE HOURS

6 A.M.

Every morning lean thine arms upon the windowsill of heaven, then with the vision in thine heart turn to meet the day.

Source Unknown

It may be the light, or birds singing, the sound of traffic or the striking of a clock, but the realization dawns that a new day is at hand—a day in which to be made glad, a day to live effectively. It is a sensitive time, this borderland between the long sleep of night and the immediacy of day: one has been left behind, the other has not fully arrived. Ideas that have been at work in the mind may be clearer now than at any other time; but they are fragile, fleeting, and can easily be lost. Take the first moments when emerging from sleep to be still, to let waking come gently, to cherish the thoughts that are hovering, to let the idea that may soon need to be acted upon gather fullness.

This is the windowsill of heaven, and for many a person whose life is committed and involved these first moments can be the least disturbed of the whole day. This is a time to keep an appointment with God, in praise and thanksgiving; the time for self-dedication and inward listening: "What do you have for me to do this day? All that I am I offer to you. Use me, in small tasks or large. May I be sensitive to the needs of others. May I be willing to do the work that is mine to do."

Over the edge of time there may come a whisper, a nudge. Light breaks into the mind as it breaks over the world. Hear, heed, be ready to respond.

Father, light up the small duties of this day's life; may they shine with the beauty of thy countenance. May we believe that glory may dwell in the commonest task of every day.

St. Augustine

7 A.M.

I wake up in the morning, and I like to begin the day by thinking what life is about, rather than plunging into the sort of things one is going to have to do. So I like to read the Gospels, the Epistles, St. Augustine, the metaphysical poets like George Herbert . . . I read a bit, and then my mind dwells on what I've read, and this I consider to be prayer.

Malcolm Muggeridge

The quietness of early morning has begun to move into the busyness of day. There are sounds that have their own meaning—voices, footsteps, clatter, traffic. The day is at hand with demands to which we will respond according to the way our lives are lived, in the quick pace of the city, the easier pace of the country. A journey is before us with events for which plans have already been made, and there will be several unplanned hours. I think of the American Indian guide who was leading a group through high mountain country. Before leaving the campsite, he walked away to stand silently beside a tree. His gaze was directed ahead to the trail they would all soon be following. Some sections of it he could see, but when it dipped into the valley, crossed a stream and went up a distant slope he could follow it only in anticipation. In silence he prepared himself for what was visible and for what was unseen. When he felt ready, he signalled to the group to follow him.

What will this day hold? Many of its demands are well known, many of its events have long been scheduled. There will be beauty and joy, there could be pain and sorrow; there will be familiar faces and new acquaintances. To be ready is to be acceptant; and to be truly acceptant is to handle creatively whatever may appear.

O God, stay with me; let no word cross my lips that is not your word, no thoughts enter my mind that are not your thoughts, no deed ever be done or entertained by me that is not your deed. Amen.

Malcolm Muggeridge

 A.M.

Be thou my vision this day. I seek Thy vision not for tomorrow, not for some future day when I am more worthy and more prepared to know and understand. I seek Thy vision **this day.** *Grant to me the flooding of my whole self with the light of Thy countenance that I may know directly when I have missed the way—when I have drifted out of the channel of Thy Purpose.*

Howard Thurman

A loved and wise physician, Sir William Osler, had a long life of service and accomplishment. His days were full, the demands on his time were many, but he had a secret which enabled him to keep his time in balance. It was a secret which he gladly shared. As a young medical student with worries about his future, he had come upon Carlyle's words, "Our main business is not to see what lies dimly at a distance, but to do what lies clearly at hand." The words became for him a practical approach which he later described as "life in daytight compartments." Living for and in each day as it came along, doing the work he was trained to do as it presented itself, finishing one task before going on to the next, he gained his mastery of time. Hurry was as unknown to him as was boredom.

To be fully present where we are, to be fully keyed to what we are doing, frees us from servitude to the past and the harassment of the future. This day, this moment of time, is all that has been given us, all that really concerns us. To embrace it as we do the light that reveals it is to respond to its needs, its duties, and its possibilities.

God, you have given me life, strength, will and this day in which to use them. May I be ever mindful that the hours come from you as a loan so that, at day's end, I may give them back to you with satisfaction and thanksgiving.

E.Y.

9 A.M.

Christ has no body now on earth but yours, no hands but yours, no feet but yours; yours are the eyes through which Christ's compassion looks out on the world, yours are the feet with which he is to go about doing good, and yours are the hands with which he is to bless us now.

St. Teresa

Doors are opening: doors to schools, offices, stores; doors to duty, to adventure. Demands are being met; routine is being faced. Anticipate as we may what we are going to find when we go through some particular door, we can never be sure of what may come through that door to us.

A friend of mine has a collie who alerts joyously to the word "Come." When directed to him, it may mean any of several good things—his food, a walk, attention; when heard in conversation by others it indicates that something of interest is on the way. "Spring is going to come soon," he heard his master say one morning and promptly took up his watch at the window near the door. Whatever the arrival might be, he would be there in greeting. It meant nothing to him that the outer world was still white with winter. Ears alert, tail poised, he was ready to welcome whatever came to the door.

We know some of the events and people that can be counted on to come through the open door of our day, but we do not know all. It is good to be ready to receive a blessing or to be a blessing, welcoming to house and heart the usual, the unexpected, the difficult, the dear.

O God, make the door of this house wide enough to receive all who need human love and fellowship, narrow enough to shut out all envy, pride and strife. Make its threshold smooth enough to be no stumbling-block to children, nor to straying feet, but rugged and strong enough to turn back the tempter's power. God, make the door of this house the gateway to thine eternal kingdom.

On the door of St. Stephen's in London

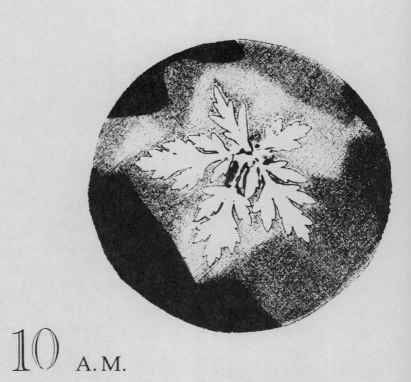

10 A.M.

True quiet means keeping still when the time has come to keep still, and going forward when the time has come to go forward. In this way rest and movement are in agreement with the demands of the time, and thus there is light in life.

The I Ching

I think of a wheel, of the way the spokes go from the hub to the rim; however small, however large, or constructed for whatever purpose, the pattern is the same. I see it as a pattern of our relationship to God and to God's creation. The nearer the spokes come to the center, the nearer they come to each other. Openness to the Presence of God does not take us away from the world but rather draws us more toward that which is the true Center and Source of all we encounter in life. The more present we are to the Center, the more we are able to be present to the all. Then I think of the sun and of how the rays emanate from it. With the wheel, movement is toward the center; with the sun, movement flows outward and life responds to it. In God's universe of light, each one has a part to play, a contribution to make.

"By reverence for life," Albert Schweitzer wrote, "we become in profound, elemental and vital fashion, devout." Living in the light, our time—no matter how pressured it may be—is precious; our acts—no matter how ordinary they may be—are sacramental. Does it matter what I do so long as I see what my relationship is to God and to the whole of God's creation?

Father, may I so live the life of love this day that all those with whom I have anything to do may be as sure of love in the world as they are of the sunlight.

E.Y.

11 A.M.

For more and more am I unwilling to make my gratitude to [God] what is commonly called "a Thanksgiving for mercies," . . . *Instead of this I would have it be gratitude for all that belongs to my life and being. For joy and sorrow, for health and sickness, for success and disappointment, for virtue and for temptation, for life and death; because I believe that all is meant for good.*

Orville Dewey

Is it really possible to praise God for everything?

A minister in Birmingham, England, Bryan Green, tells this story about his aunt in his book *Saints Alive*. "On one occasion she was hurrying to catch a train at Paddington Station. Arriving dead on time she found the barrier gate slammed in her face. Out loud she ejaculated, beaming all over her face, 'Never mind. Praise the Lord.' Then she went off to get a cup of tea. On returning for the next train, the ticket collector said, 'Excuse me, Ma'am. What was that you said when I slammed the door in your face half an hour ago?' 'I don't remember,' she replied. 'It sounded strange to me. Did you say something like "Praise the Lord?"' My aunt paused a moment, and then answered, 'Yes, I expect I did. I do praise him. I am sure it is quite all right that I missed the train, and God has some purpose for me through it.' To her surprise the ticket collector asked, 'Would you mind missing another train, because I should like to speak to you after this one has gone.' So she missed another train, and he told her his story, the story of a marriage breaking up, of his longing for help, and before she caught her train she had helped him to put his faith in Christ, and later to put his marriage right."

Enter into his gates with thanksgiving; and into his courts with praise.

Psalm 100:4

Noon

Do as little children, who with one hand held fast by their father, and with the other gather Strawberries or Mulberries along the hedges: So you, gathering and managing the Affairs of this World with one hand, with the other hold fast the Hand of your Heavenly Father, turning yourself toward him from time to time to see if your employments be pleasing to him. And take heed above all things that you have not let go his Hand and his Protection.

St. Francis de Salès

The sun has reached its zenith. The journey now is westward. It has been a climb from darkness to light; it will be a descent from light to darkness. But the change will be subtle and not soon noticed. Twelve strokes resounding inwardly or through the air signal a pause in work, a time for refreshment.

And it is needed, not alone for the rest or the food, but for a change in the depth of focus. The eyes of the mind need to shift from the outer to the inner view, from human personalities to the Christ in every man. When the journey is resumed, the step will be more resilient, the eye clearer.

An ancient Irish rune tells of a stranger passed on the road. Food and drink were made ready, and there was welcome in the heart should the stranger stop at the croft. He did, and all were blessed; not only those who served and spoke with him, but the cattle and the small children at their play, and the old folk who sat nodding by the fire. "And the lark said in her song, 'Often, often, often goes the Christ in the stranger's guise.' "

Christ be the head of this house,
The unseen guest at every meal,
The unseen listener to every conversation.
                    Words on an old sampler

1 P.M.

Cheered by the presence of God, I will do each moment, without anxiety, according to the strength which he shall give me, the work which his providence assigns me.

Francois de Fénelon

I have met people today whose very being in the world at the same time that I am in it has delighted me. The words we have exchanged have been good, stimulating or comforting, and I have felt enriched. I have met others with whom this has not been so. I have felt irked, bothered by their words and have had no desire for their company. But I cannot get away from the fact that love is at the heart of the universe; to love is as much a necessity as it is a command.

If I take one of the difficult people and mentally give myself to that person, something is bound to happen. By an exercise of the imagination, I picture myself with that person on a desert island waiting for the turn of the tide, or sheltered in a mountain hut while a storm rages. To survive, each one of us must come to the other's aid. In discovering ourselves as we really are, in the urgency that has been forced upon us, we make room for love to happen. Perhaps the secret is that when response is made as if to a behest from God, a way is opened to let love in. Then the miracle: the realization that love *is*. It can be relied upon to do its work as the sun can be relied upon to shine.

One instance, one exercise: and what if this were carried further? What if every day such an effort were made, not with an imagined situation but on the street, in the office, at home?

In every man there is a king. Speak to the king and the king will come forth.

Scandinavian Proverb

2 P.M.

Imagine a man whose business hounds him through many streets and across the market-place the livelong day. He almost forgets that there is a Maker of the world. Only when the time for the Afternoon Prayer comes, does he remember: 'I must pray.' And then, from the bottom of his heart, he heaves a sigh of regret that he has spent his day on vain and idle matters, and he runs into a by-street and stands there, and prays. God holds him dear, very dear and his prayer pierces the firmament.

Israel Ben Eliezer

A friend of mine has a loving practice. Every day, as time allows, she goes into a church that she passes on the way to or from her office. There she spends a few moments in prayer, not for her own needs and not for her own friends and family, but specifically for those who have no one to pray for them. She asks for nothing, but she holds them in the light, seeing them as within the circle of God's care, and responding to God's good will for them. With some true touch established, her heart as it reaches out enfolds the unknown as it does the dear and the familiar.

It was the custom of the voyageurs, those hardy canoe men of the seventeenth century paddling through the waters of the Canadian wilderness, to pray often: at the beginning of a hazardous day, at its safe conclusion, and on the journey itself. Each made his supplication, but it was never for himself. It was for the man who sat beside him in the canoe, or behind him, or before him. Free to devote himself to others, the voyageur knew that there was always someone who would be praying for him.

Almighty God, we entrust all who are dear to us to thy never-failing care and love, for this life and the life to come; knowing that thou art doing for them better things than we can desire or pray for.
                          The Book of Common Prayer

3 P. M.

'Tis God gives skill,
But not without men's hands: He could not make
Antonio Stradivari's violins
Without Antonio.

George Eliot

   Caught up in the movement of the day, I have
listened to many voices, heard many words, been
a part of many conversations. Now, I would take
part in a silent conversation, something that can
only be when listening is done without interrup-

tion, when listening is total. What I hear may fill me so that there will be no need to answer in words, but in action.

So, I have taken myself in imagination to a hilltop where I see things in a different light. A yearning toward God that is as simple as breathing has taken hold of me, for the hill is an altar and the offering is myself. Often I ask for something—the solution to a problem, the answer to a need, but not now. In a quiet of my own making, in a silence of my own seeking, I ask as directly as I would of a companion standing beside me, "What can I do for you?" Waiting, I free my mind from thinking but keep it attentive. And I know that this receptivity, this hospitality, is prayer.

The answer may come soon or late, but it comes in time, and it is an idea in the mind. Perhaps it is something that could be done, should be done; nurturing it, it becomes something that must be done. The intimation is not to be denied, nor is it to be deferred. Leaving the highlands of the spirit for the lowlands of service, I know that I am not alone.

We and God have business with each other; and in opening ourselves to his influence our deepest destiny is fulfilled.

William James

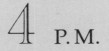

4 P.M.

To yield is to be preserved whole.
To be bent is to become straight.
To be empty is to be full.
To be worn out is to be renewed.

The Way of Lao Tzu

Today at tea time I had a friend with me, in the form of a book taken down from the shelf. Turning the pages, I came to a marked paragraph and read slowly. It is as though Mary K. Smith is herself present and speaking to me:

"Prayer is an exercise of the spirit, as thought is of the mind. To pray about anything is to use the powers of our spirit on it, just as to think clearly is to use our mental powers. For the best solution of every problem, the best carrying out of every action, both thought and prayer are necessary . . . To pray about any day's work does not mean to ask for success in it. It means, first, to realise my own inability to do even a familiar job, as it truly should be done, unless I am in touch with eternity, unless I do it 'unto God', unless I have the Father with me. It means to see 'my' work as part of a whole, to see 'myself' as not mattering much, but my faith, the energy, will and striving, which I put into the work, as mattering a great deal. My faith is the point in me at which God comes into my work; through faith the work is given dignity and value. And if, through some weakness of mine, or fault of others, or just 'unavoidable circumstances', the work seems a failure, yet prayer is not wasted when it is unanswered, any more than love is wasted when it is unreturned."

Father, I thank thee that thou hast heard me, and I knew that thou hearest me always.

John 11:41-42

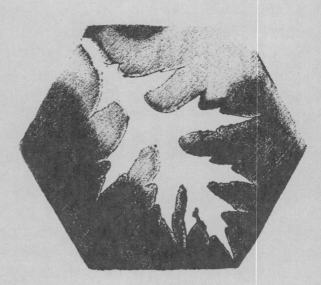

5 P.M.

The Christian prays in every situation, in his walks for recreation, in his dealings with others, in silence, in reading, in all rational pursuits. And although he is only thinking of God in the little chamber of the soul, and calling upon his Father with silent aspirations, God is near him and with him while he is yet speaking.

St. Clement of Alexandria

As the hours move on and the reminder to pray recurs, something becomes ever more real: that prayer is not asking God to intercede in daily affairs but that it is a recognition of oneness with God. Realizing the presence is to know that all who are held close in heart and dear in memory are also in the presence. Once it might have seemed that a special place, time, method were requisite for prayer; now it is becoming clear that there is no place where God is not, no time that is not God's, and the way may simply be that of thoughts tendered and tendering.

C. S. Lewis says "We may ignore, but we can nowhere evade, the presence of God. The world is crowded with him. He walks everywhere *incognito*. And the *incognito* is not always hard to penetrate. The real labor is to remember, to attend." Humbling and exalting, startling yet reasonable, is the realization that we are the means through which God works, the means through which his purposes of good are accomplished. It does not matter how small our deeds may be, or how insignificant the part may seem that we are given to play. The fine line of cement that holds together the bricks in a wall is scarcely discernible, but without it there would be no wall.

O, may I be to the Lord as a man's right hand is to him!

Source Unknown

6 P.M.

When the dawn appears,
When the light grows,
When midday burns,
When has ceased the holy light,
When the clear night comes;
I sing your praises, O Father,
Healer of hearts,
Healer of bodies,
Giver of wisdom,
Remedy of evil.

Synesius of Cyrene

Time has been filled in the busyness of the day, and it has often been hurried. We have felt ourselves to be small parts of a large multitude embarked on the adventure of living. As such, we are one with all creation—people, animals, plants, stars—"bound in the bundle of life" and responding in our various ways. George MacDonald, in one of the briefest of his prayers, said, "Pray to the God of sparrows and rabbits and men, who never lets anyone out of his ken." Aware or not as we may have been of this during the day, we have never been out of that ken.

Now, time is taking on a different aspect. It is less hurried, less elusive. Doors that opened several hours ago have started to close, and different doors are opening. The journey of the day that led into work and activity has turned to the quieter things of home. And for thoughts, too, it is a time of ingathering. The first star may already have appeared in the western sky. Seeing it, there are some who wish on it, and in a way a wish is kin to a prayer.

Evening star, you bring all things which the bright dawn has scattered: you bring sheep, you bring the goat, you bring the child back to its mother.

Sappho   Fragment 1

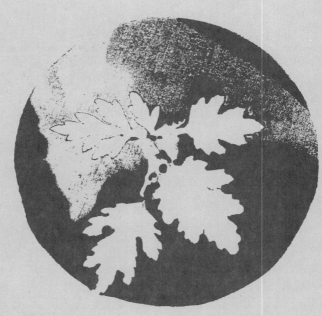

7 P.M.

When his life's work was threatened, St. Ignatius Loyola was asked what he would do if Pope Paul IV dissolved or otherwise acted against the Society of Jesus, to which he had devoted his energy and gifts; and he replied: "I would pray for fifteen minutes, then I would not think of it again."

Alan Paton

Much has been right with the day and yet now there is a surge of feeling that nothing has been right. I have allowed people to disturb me; disappointment and dissatisfaction have nibbled away the edge of my composure. I don't know what to do. I am in a fog.

Fog, yes.

Once, in a row boat with a friend and well out from shore, fog closed us in. The water had a smooth surface, the air was damp and motionless. We should have been able to hear the hollow tinkling of the bell buoys that would have guided us into and through the channel, but in the stillness they were still too. Using the oars hard and making the boat turn clockwise, then counter clockwise, we made ripples and kept making them until the ripples reached to the buoys, rocking them so they began to sound. The sound guided us to safe haven.

Remembering this, the tension of the day began to yield.

When you get to your wit's end, you'll find God lives there.

Old Saying

8 P.M.

Come now, little man! Flee for a while from your tasks, hide yourself for a little space from the turmoil of your thoughts. Come, cast aside your burdensome cares, and put aside your laborious pursuits. . . . Give your time to God, and rest in him for a little while. Enter into the inner chamber of your mind, shut out all things save God . . . and having barred the door of your chamber, seek him.

Anselm of Canterbury

The day has been lent to me in the same way that my life has. How has it been used? In the freshness and vigor of morning, I wondered what the day might hold; in the tranquility of evening, there is another kind of wondering. Through the work that has been done, the people encountered, the journeys made, love has been set in motion. Is this the answer when we question the reason for existence or the purpose behind life?

It is too early to have a full accounting, for there are still sands of time to run through the hour glass of the day, but it is not too early to look ahead. Another day will offer another opportunity. There is comfort in the ancient Irish charm which names three holy things against which evil has no power: the merciful word, the singing word, the good word.

How often we hear the words: "Have a good day." Pleasant as the words are, they can fall on the ear without heed because of their frequency. Early today I was startled into attention at a gas station when the cheerful words that sent me on my way were, "Give a good day." Did I?

Search me, O God, and know my heart; Try me and know my thoughts. See if there be any wicked way in me, and lead me in the way everlasting.
Psalm 139:23,24

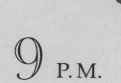

9 P.M.

Do not be concerned about what may happen tomorrow. The Eternal Father who has cared for you today will take care of you tomorrow, and every day. Either he will shield you from suffering or send you unfailing strength with which to bear it. So be of good heart and cast aside all anxious thoughts and images.

St. Francis de Sales

The morning was a time of dedication; the evening is one of surrender. Whether the day has been burdened or beautiful, pressured or free, it can now be turned over to God. "I am not afraid of tomorrow," William Allen White said, "For I have known yesterday, and loved today." Looking back over the day, there are bound to be many reasons to love it.

Tasks have been accomplished, discoveries have been made. There may have been frustrations and disappointments, but they have been part of the ongoing day. There are moments that can be remembered with a little inward leap of joy: an exchange of words that prompted a new way of thinking, the arrival of a long-awaited letter, a smile from a stranger bringing the realization that we are all more closely related than we are often ready to admit. There was a glimpse of something so lovely that it called for a moment of worship. A long piece of work was brought to completion. An old friend was seen. A new friend was made. A misunderstanding was healed. And, from the difficult events, something that may prove to be of enduring value has been learned. Seeing them in the light of evening brings a thanksgiving which is, in itself, a form of renewal for another day's adventure.

Round our skiff be God's aboutness
Ere she try the deeps of sea,
Sea-shell frail for all her stoutness
Unless Thou her helmsman be.

Hebridean Altars

10 P.M.

Thy body was given thee to be a lantern only to the candle of love that shineth in thy soul.

Thomas Traherne

"The physical structure of man," is the basic definition of the body, but it has been referred to in more visual ways. St. Paul speaks of "earthen vessels," St. Francis de Sales calls it "Brother Ass," and a contemporary sees it as "a useful vehicle for the advancing spiritual idea." I like Traherne's metaphor of a candle in a lantern. As the tender of the lamp keeps it in good condition that its light may shine, so we have a like responsibility to be kind to the physical body. Bless it. It has a way to go, a work to do before it can be exchanged for a spiritual body.

Tiredness has taken over. Muscles and limbs have served well and are ready for a rest. Yield to these needs and respect them, taking a hint from the work of nature. Birds have snuggled into their nests, animals have tucked themselves into their burrows; it is time to cozy ourselves for awhile in a chair with a satisfying book, or in bed to wait for sleep. Cervantes, who wrapped up wise counsel in easy-going words, said about sleep that "It covers a man all over, thoughts and all, like a cloak; 'tis meat for the hungry, drink for the thirsty, heat for the cold, and cold for the hot." But, before drifting off, save a moment for a prayer.

O, Great Spirit, whose voice I hear in the winds and whose breath gives life to the world, hear me! I come before you, one of your many children. I am small and weak. I need your strength and wisdom. . . . Make me wise, so that I may know the things you have taught my people, the lesson you have hidden in leaf and rock. I seek strength, not to be superior to my brothers, but to be able to fight my greatest enemy—myself. Make me ever ready to come to you with clean hands and straight eyes, so that when my life fades, as a fading sunset, my spirit may come to you without shame.

An old Ute Indian prayer

11 P.M.

In meditation let the person rouse himself from things temporal, and let him collect himself within himself—that is to say, within the very center of his soul, where lies impressed the very image of God. Here let him hearken to the voice of God as though speaking to him from on high, yet present in his soul, as though there were no other voice in the world save God and himself.

San Pedro de Alcantara

What, of all that has happened today or of the little that has happened, has given satisfaction? Who, of the people encountered, linger happily in memory? This is no time to dwell upon the disturbing, the unattained, the imperfect. To do so would be to find sleep elusive. By an act of will that which may have marred the day must be given over to God to enable thinking to be anchored fast in that which is good. Rest will come then, and with it the restoration that is sleep.

During those last hours in the garden, alone and wrestling mightily within himself, Jesus met the test of prayer when he could say at last to his Father, "Not my will, but thine be done." It was then that an angel came to strengthen him. Our struggles are not comparable to his, but the test is the same. We meet it when we set self aside and trustfully turn to God with a readiness to be shown: "Not my will, but thine." The way is open for the angel to come.

O holy Spirit of God, visit now this soul of mine and tarry within it . . . Lodge in my will's most inward citadel and order all my doings . . . And give me grace at all times to rejoice in thy mysterious companionship.
John Baillie

Midnight

While all things were wrapped in peaceful silence and night was in the midst of its swift course . . . a secret word leaped down from heaven, to me . . . Because the same One, who is begotten and born of God the Father, without ceasing in eternity, is born today, within time, in human nature, we make a holiday to celebrate it. . . . This birth is always happening. And yet, if it does not occur in me, how could it help me? Everything depends on that.

Meister Eckhart

The hands of the clock have come together in the classic position of prayer. Seeing them so, makes me bring my hands together, fingertips touching, palms slightly apart. There is serenity in the gesture, as if need were cupped in the assurance of answer.

Midnight is a time of marvel, a time of wonder. In legend and song and often-told story, miraculous events were associated with a particular midnight when a Child was born in Bethlehem: a star shone, flowers bloomed, creatures knelt in adoration and some were given the gift of speech.

What does this mean but that awareness, awakened by a great happening, goes beyond human perceiving. Words become inadequate, while the heart in pondering finds its own manner of expression. The angels that herald birth sing on, and rebirth is a continuum. Let wonder have its way, if only for the moment that the hands come together in prayer.

Let each man think himself an act of God,
His mind a thought,
His life a breath of God;
And let each try,
By great thoughts and good deeds,
To show the most of Heaven he hath in him.
Philip James Bailey

1 A.M.

If one should give me a dish of sand and tell me that
there were particles of iron in it, I might look for them
with my eyes and search for them with my clumsy
fingers and never detect them; but let me take a magnet
and sweep through that dish of sand and that magnet
would draw those tiny particles of iron to it through the
power of the magnet's attraction. The unthankful heart
is like my finger in the sand, it discovers no mercies; but
let the thankful heart sweep through the day, and, as
the magnet finds the iron, so it will find in every hour
some heavenly blessing; only the iron in God's hand is
gold.

Henry Ward Beecher

Some say a cup of camomile tea or a warm bath can induce relaxation, but gratitude is the great wooer of sleep. Although new ideas surge for expression, or worrisome thoughts knock insistently at the mind's door, it is good to leave them to themselves for awhile. They will not be lost, only clearer when the time of waking comes. In sleep we go deep into the ground of our being, and there much is worked on in mysterious ways. Clarity may come with the morning, or illumination may come in a dream as it crosses the invisible borderline between consciousness and slumber. If this happens, receive and remember, so upon waking its significance may be related to the ideas seeking the release of form and action. The guise may seem strange, the language may require interpretation, but through the ages God has often spoken in dreams, and men and women have profited by heeding.

He giveth his beloved sleep.

Psalm 127:2

2 A.M.

We are evidently in the midst of a process, and the slowness of God's processes in the material world prepares us, or ought to prepare us, for something analogous in the moral world; so that at least we may be allowed to trust that he who has taken untold ages for the formation of a bit of old red sandstone may not be limited to threescore years and ten for the perfecting of a human spirit.

Thomas Erskine of Linlathen

Quiet abounds. In the gradual slowing down that has come over the world of nature and people, the minutes seem to move more deliberately than during the day. But time and its tide go on. The pressures that have beset the busy hours have given way to deeper sensations: lying awake, one sees more clearly in the dark, feels more intensely in the aloneness. A single hour takes a long time to pass, but living in it is discipleship for eternity.

It was one of the medieval mystics who said, "He who is in a hurry delays the things of God." This is what the quietness is saying in itself: the dawn cannot be hurried, nor can the seasons. A seed stirs, a bud unfolds, a leaf falls, each in a sequence long established and in its own time. As we move with the order of events we are part of the great ongoing progression of mankind; one step at a time, one hour, one year, one decade, moving from birth to death, with life the means to the end. The continuity that links events and makes process and performance one is the direction: Godward.

God, who a thousand years doth wait
To work a thousandth part of thy great plan,
In me create
A humble, patient heart.

George MacDonald

3 A.M.

Let mystery have its place in you; do not be always turning up your whole soil with the plowshare of self-examination, but leave a little fallow corner in your heart ready for any seed the winds may bring, and reserve a nook of shadow for the passing bird; keep a place in your heart for the unexpected guests, an altar for the unknown God.

Henri Frederic Amiel

Something has roused me—the clock? a noise? a need? Or was it the nagging remembrance of a task undone during the day or to be done tomorrow? Things tend to loom large in the darkness and sleep does not readily return; but this is no time to fret about the past or be bothered about the future. It is a time to cherish the present. It is rare, this hour of solitariness; it can be a source of creative power.

Go back over the day and lift thought in prayer for each person encountered since early morning. Perhaps one of the many is awake, praying too, and some mystical link will be forged. There are those who have no one to pray for them, and there are some who have forgotten how to pray. Prayer comforts and calms; taking away the burden or the responsibility, it places it under God's care.

Lie still and let the night enfold you. If the oblivion of sleep does not return easily, remember that a body at rest with the mind at peace is still renewing itself. What is gained in solitude will soon have an opportunity to be given out in service.

Let nothing disturb thee,
Nothing affright thee.
All things are passing,
  God never changeth.
Patience gains all things.
Who hath God wanteth nothing.
  Alone God sufficeth.

St. Teresa of Avila

4 A.M.

The future glory of the Resurrection begins in this life, as a hidden seed planted in the ground, as a spring of living water raised from a deep well. This inner, present vitality, Jesus taught, is connected with the future glory not in just some nominal or conventional fashion, like a ticket of admission to a play or a dance. It is organically **one with it.** The new life begins now, right here in the midst of this changing and transient world.

John LaFarge

The silence is so intense that the striking of a distant clock comes into it like sounds from another world. How bright the stars are! How still the trees! Neither branches nor leaves are in motion. Everything seems to be waiting for something to happen. It is a time when the veil between the worlds is thin. There seems neither space nor time between the unseen and the seen. I am aware, as never during the day, of the threshold leading from life to greater life, for all creation as for me. Assurance becomes reassurance. Words of Socrates come into my mind, "Nothing can harm a good man in this world or the next."

In the holy stillness, I think of death; not with fear or longing but with expectancy as a time of ingathering. If I have felt at home in this life, shall I not feel even more so in the life to come? If I have lived fully here, shall I not live even more fully in the continuation?

Be with me, Lord. Keep me beyond all prayers:
For more than all my prayers my need of thee,
And thou beyond all need, all unknown cares;
What the heart's dear imagination dares,
Thou dost transcend in measureless majesty
All prayers in one—my God, be unto me
Thy own eternal self, absolutely.

George MacDonald

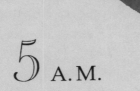

5 A.M.

To the Celt each new day is a gift, a flower; above all, a mystery which calls for the companionship of God if a man would see it well through. Hence the old prayer: God be with me in this, thy day, every day and every way, with me and for me, in this, thy day.

Hebridean Altars

Something is happening around me: the dark is less dark, the silence is less deep. Even the air is changing. It is damper, sweeter. Morning is at hand. Light will soon come flowing over the edge of the world, bringing with it the day. What a gift! Whether wrapped in streamers of color or folded in tissues of mist, it will be mine to use in ways that I can foresee and in those that are unexpected. The day will make its own revelation, bring its own challenge; my part will be to respond with joy and readiness.

There is an old saying that a good man greets every day as if it were a holiday. Those five strokes of the clock that scattered the silence were a call to be alert for whatever the day has in store: its duties, its routines, its unknown experience; a new adventure awaits me. The day may be no different from any other, or it may be very different. Whatever it brings, it comes with the dawn and it is mine.

All shall be well, and all shall be well, and all manner of things shall be well.

Julian of Norwich

Afterword

What has it meant, this discipline of the day? This exercise of prayer, this inner journey? A closer walk with God and a deepening realization that one is always *at one* with God?

Often, walking in the woods, I have cupped my hands to a spring and drunk water flowing from within the earth. It has a different taste from any water out of tap or container, and its quality has been not only refreshing but revivifying. So, as the return to the Source is made, the effect is revivifying: work is more rewarding, play more satisfying, love is more readily expressed and warmly received, worship is more spontaneous.

Even in the conscious awareness of the striking of the hour, there has been a timelessness. An artist knows no limit to time until the work undertaken has been completed. Even so, the one who dedicates the hours to God makes of each day a work of art.